DEDICATION

To my dear old friends, who will likely
recognize themselves in the Tea Ladies.
To my daughter, Jen, who caught the vision
and helped me capture their personalities.
To my sons, who have always believed I could
do it. To my new friends, especially Ruthie,
who inspired these endearing characters.
And in memory of my wonderful mother,
Grace, who almost lived long enough to see it
happen, and whose grandchildren lovingly
nicknamed her "Minty."

Good Friends Sip Together Through Thick and Thin,
a title in the Tea Ladies Collection™
Text © 2001 by Dee Appel, Heartfelt Lines
Published by Blue Cottage Gifts™,
a division of Multnomah Publishers, Inc.®
P.O. Box 1720, Sisters, OR 97759

ISBN: 1-58860-000-9

Artwork designs by Gay Talbott Boassy are
reproduced under license from the publisher ©Arts
Uniq', Inc.®, Cookeville, TN, and may not be reproduced without permission. For information regarding
art prints featured in this book, please contact:

    Arts Uniq', Inc.
    P.O. Box 3085
    Cookeville, TN 38502
    1-800-223-5020

Designed by:
Koechel Peterson & Associates, Minneapolis, MN

Multnomah Publishers Inc. has made every effort to
trace the ownership of all poems and quotes. In the
event of a question arising from the use of a poem
or quote, we regret any error made and will be
pleased to make the necessary correction in future
editions of this book.

Scripture quotations are taken from
The Holy Bible, King James Version (KJV).

Printed in China

01 02 03 04 05 06—10 9 8 7 6 5 4 3 2 1 0

www.gift-talk.com

Good Friends Sip Together

THROUGH THICK AND THIN

Written by DEE APPEL

Illustrated by GAY TALBOTT BOASSY

Good Friends Sip Together
THROUGH THICK AND THIN

Friends are like tea cups—a special collection,
Some aged by use and timely affection.
Some are still new, they sparkle and shine,
And some are robust, like a glass of fine wine.
Others are dainty and easy to shatter,
Their care and feeding's a delicate matter.
Some friends are sturdy, and ask very little,
And others are rigid and just a bit brittle.
But best friends are loyal, and always have been, 'cause
Good Friends Sip Together Through Thick and Thin.

A FRIEND IS WHAT
THE HEART NEEDS
ALL THE TIME.

HENRY VAN DYKE

DARJEELING

Darjie was born with
The proverbial spoon.
She's always, yes always
Impeccably groomed.
I swear she wakes up
With her lipstick untouched....
Though I love her to pieces,
She can be a bit much!
She's dripping with diamonds
And dressed in Dior.
She'll talk your ear off
And come back for more.
She greets me with "Dahling"—
She's slightly affected....
But from well-heeled parties,
She's never rejected.

Darjie,
Dahling

Her driver, named Murphy,

Has learned through the years

He once cracked the window

And reduced her to tears.

Her flaming red hair

Was disturbed

just a touch....

When it comes

to her hairdo,

She can't

handle much.

Darjie helped me out one time
When finances were tight
And never told another soul,
Although I thought she might.
She always knows the latest news
And keeps me up to date,
And I can set my clock by her....
She's never, ever late.
She's always heading something up
And always on the go.
She's headed up the blood drive here
for six years in a row.
If you need work, she knows someone
—her father's Uncle Tim—
She'll call up the whole world for you
Until she locates him.

A FRIEND LOVES AT ALL TIMES....

PROVERBS 17:17

Lately I have noticed
Just a few things start to change.
Darjie might forget a word—
For her that's very strange!
One minute she is freezing,
The next she says she's hot....
I suggested it's the change of life....
She said, "It's certainly NOT!"
She does have one weakness
From what I have seen.
It's her poodle, named "Strudle"—
He's small, and he's mean!
She takes that dog everywhere—
He's spoiled ROTTEN, too!
But we have to ignore it,
'Cause that's what friends do.

WHERE

THERE

ARE

FRIENDS,

THERE IS

WEALTH.

TITUS PLAUTUS

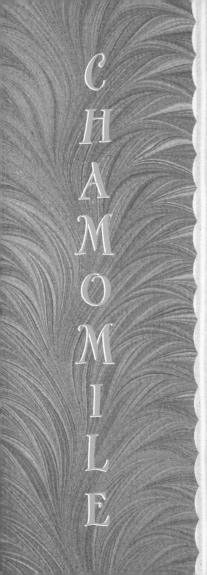

CHAMOMILE

Cammie came into our lives
Three years ago or more.
She was helping out the Girl Scouts
By going door to door.
Draped in a dress of strange off-red,
Belted at the waist,
With an equally awful crocheted belt—
I knew she had no taste.
So there she was at my door
Selling sweet confections.
I later learned she'd lost her way
And wouldn't ask directions.
Something dear about her
Made me ask her to come in,
And then before I knew it,
We seemed like long-lost friends.

My Friend
Cammie

Cammie drives us crazy

With the things she has to save.

If you ever give her anything,

She'll take it to her grave!

Her attic's stacked from roof to floor,

Her garage is overflowing....

Some things have been there so long

That mold is actually growing!

The other day she called up Jazz

And asked if she had room

For just a couple "somethings"—

some favorite heirlooms.

Her last attempt to clean things out

Was back in sixty-five.

She actually boxed up quite a bit
For the local clothing drive.
She drove down to the parking lot—
That's as far as she could go.
Of course she had to bring it back,
"Just in case," you know?
We've tried and tried to give advice
If she would only heed it....
But she can't bring herself to throw it out
'Cause somebody might need it!!!
Cammie is our comfort friend,
She wants to make life better,
And she would take your pain for you
If God would only let her.
She always knows just what to say
To help a suffering soul,

OUR EMOTIONS

TWO PERSONS
CANNOT LONG
BE FRIENDS
IF THEY CANNOT
FORGIVE EACH
OTHERS
LITTLE FAILINGS.

JEAN DE LA BRUYERE

And making our lives easier
Seems her lifelong goal.
Cammie puddles up a lot—
She's awfully sentimental,
She's sure to cry at Hallmark cards
Because she is so gentle.
Darjie's tried to help her
With her slightly unkempt hair.
And Cammie really, really tries,
But she frankly doesn't care.
It's not "her thing" to be well-coiffed,
She'd rather plant a flower
Or listen to a friend's great need
For hour after hour.
She will definitely enchant you
With her captivating smile....
It helps us overlook her hair
And impossible lack of style.

A

CONSTANT

FRIEND

IS A

THING

RARE

AND

HARD

TO

FIND.

PLUTARCH HARD

WE CAN NEVER

REPLACE A FRIEND.

WHEN A MAN IS

FORTUNATE ENOUGH

TO HAVE SEVERAL,

HE FINDS THEY ARE

ALL DIFFERENT.

NO ONE HAS

A DOUBLE

IN FRIENDSHIP.

JOHANN SCHILLER

©Gay Talbott Boassy

J
A
S
M
I
N
E

Jasmine is the kind of friend
Who always loves a party.
She's full of life and vinegar,
And her constitution's hardy.
Her zesty laugh and zany ways
Will always draw you in.
She considers you a friend of hers
Even if you've never been.
She often wears a yellow dress—
She's always very snazzy.
She loves to laugh and dance and sing—
Her close friends call her "Jazzie."
She generously uses flowery scent—
Sometimes it overpowers.
And you can tell she's been there
When she's been gone for hours!

Jazzie
Jasmine

Jazzie has to struggle

With the battle of the bulge.

Her weight's a deep, dark secret

She swears she won't divulge.

She loves to eat and that's the truth—

It truly is a curse!

She's always on a diet
And each one's getting worse!
The latest thing I think I heard
Was celery and gin—
She swears it works
and then she asks...
"Aren't I getting thin?!"
Jazzie loves to stay up late—
Far too late for me.
So when we plan a tea party,
It's always after three.
Otherwise she won't be up
Or have her usual zest,

WHEN
FRIENDS
MEET,
HEARTS
WARM.

PROVERB

And our tea is simply much more fun

When Jazzie's at her best.

Jazz can always tell a joke

And remember how it ends.

That's more than I can say

For many of my friends.

She's always optimistic

And sees the best in me.

Jazzie's just the kind of friend

That I would like to be.

THERE

CAN

BE NO

FRIENDSHIP

WHERE

THERE

IS NO

FREEDOM...

FRIENDSHIP

LOVES

FREE

AIR.

WILLIAM PENN

PEPPERMINT

I love to go to Minty's house
At any time of year.
But my favorite time to visit
Is when Christmastime is near.
A better hostess you won't find—
She's thoughtful and she's sweet.
Whenever we're together,
All I do is eat!
She's always baking goodies—
She's clever and creative—
A devoted fan of Martha S.,
And an Oregonian native.
Minty is the kind of friend
Who can never do enough.

Minty

She brings me tea and rocky road—

Makes sure my pillow's fluffed.

My slightest whim is her command,

She loves me

and it shows,

And if my heart needs a boost,

It seems she always knows.

Minty is obsessive

About a thing or two

She offers breath mints constantly—

It doesn't matter who!

And God forbid you should forget

If you ever spend the night

To bring along your toothbrush—

Though it's really quite alright.

For one entire closet

Is devoted to her guests.

TRUE

FRIENDSHIP

IS A KNOT

THAT

ANGELS

HAVE TIED.

ANONYMOUS

It's stuffed with extras of all kinds—

She only buys the best!

Minty craves the winter nights

And long chats by the fire.

Her red-striped socks and sense of fun

Are things that I admire.

She's someone I can always trust,

Whatever life may bring,

And she forgives me quickly—

She's just the sweetest thing!

FRIENDSHIP!

MYSTERIOUS

CEMENT

OF THE

SOUL!

SWEET'NER

OF LIFE...

ROBERT BLAIR

AND BE KIND TO
ONE ANOTHER,
TENDERHEARTED,
FORGIVING
ONE ANOTHER...

EPHESIANS 4:32

PEKOE

Pekoe keeps a perfect house
With everything in place.
She serves up tea and oranges
With elegance and grace.
She's the eldest of our friends,
She's tiny and she's wise,
With energy and inner strength
That belie her tiny size.
Pekoe has her own sweet charms,
She's set in her own ways,
She lives the lifestyle of her choice—
It's one of bygone days.
For one thing, she won't have a phone—
She hates them with a passion.

Pekoe
&
Orange
Pekoe

She washes all her clothes by hand—

She's just a touch old-fashioned.

We all suspect that secretly

She wants us to drop by.

It forces us to slow life down—

To sit, and sip,

and sigh.

Her yard is lush with orange trees
Their fragrance is what greets us,
And in her English garden
Is often where she seats us.
Miss Pekoe's a widow
And has been now for years
She loves us all completely
And thinks that we're all "dears."
She also has a granddaughter,
And she's her greatest pride.
"Opie's" just a little shy
And clings to Grammy's side.
Opie's growing up to be
A lovely kind of child.
She's respectful and she's charming,
With a manner that is mild.

She has a zillion nail colors,
A hundred for each season.
She'll gladly paint a new one on
If you give her a reason.
Miss Pekoe's our mentor,
Her advice is always wise.
Whenever we have problems,
She cuts them down to size.
Sometimes when I'm feeling sad,
I know just where to go—
She loves on me and gives me hugs
She lets me cry, you know?

LET US

LOVE

ONE

ANOTHER.

1 JOHN 4:7

FRIENDSHIP

IS A UNION

OF SPIRITS,

A MARRIAGE

OF HEARTS...

WILLIAM PENN

TEATIME
FOR THE
TEA LADIES

Every Sunday afternoon

Beside the willow tree,

Soothed by the setting summer sun,

We all dress up for tea.

Jazzie in her yellow dress,

With perfume head to toe,

Our hostess—such a clever girl!

She keeps us on the go!

Minty wears a striking suit,
Striped in red and white.
She smiles her sweet and radiant smile
And laughs with sheer delight.
Leisurely I stroll the lawn
In my favorite teatime gown
That sways like flax in moonlit breeze
And flows across the ground.
I pick a lonely daisy
To nestle in my hair
And tuck more in my pocket
For my friends and I to share.

I catch a glimpse of Darjie

    I guess she thinks she's late—

A flash of zany, flamy fun

    Flies past the garden gate.

Finally, we gather 'round

    Our table set with style.

Pekoe asks the blessing

    And smiles her loving smile.

Opie serves the apple scones–

As one we start to giggle.

If we keep this up,

we know for sure

We'll suffer midriff jiggle!

Just as the flavors of our tea

Change with secret blends,

We celebrate our special time

With new or

lifelong friends.

PEKOE'S
TEA BLESSING

Dear Lord, I thank You for Your grace

And for this lovely day.

I thank You for each special friend—

Lord, bless each one, I pray.

And Lord, I ask You'd bless our time,

And bless our sharing, too—

Please bless our food and bless our tea—

Bless all we say and do. Amen.